MIX
Papier aus verantwortungsvollen Quellen
Paper from responsible sources
FSC® C105338

Samuel Skipper

Assessing the Role of Globalisation in the Rise of New Right Attitudes in Germany and Italy

Anchor Academic
Publishing

Skipper, Samuel: Assessing the Role of Globalisation in the Rise of New Right
Attitudes in Germany and Italy, Hamburg, Anchor Academic Publishing 2016

Buch-ISBN: 978-3-96067-085-8
PDF-eBook-ISBN: 978-3-96067-585-3
Druck/Herstellung: Anchor Academic Publishing, Hamburg, 2016

Bibliografische Information der Deutschen Nationalbibliothek:
Die Deutsche Nationalbibliothek verzeichnet diese Publikation in der Deutschen
Nationalbibliografie; detaillierte bibliografische Daten sind im Internet über
http://dnb.d-nb.de abrufbar.

Bibliographical Information of the German National Library:
The German National Library lists this publication in the German National Bibliography.
Detailed bibliographic data can be found at: http://dnb.d-nb.de

All rights reserved. This publication may not be reproduced, stored in a retrieval system
or transmitted, in any form or by any means, electronic, mechanical, photocopying,
recording or otherwise, without the prior permission of the publishers.

Das Werk einschließlich aller seiner Teile ist urheberrechtlich geschützt. Jede Verwertung
außerhalb der Grenzen des Urheberrechtsgesetzes ist ohne Zustimmung des Verlages
unzulässig und strafbar. Dies gilt insbesondere für Vervielfältigungen, Übersetzungen,
Mikroverfilmungen und die Einspeicherung und Bearbeitung in elektronischen Systemen.

Die Wiedergabe von Gebrauchsnamen, Handelsnamen, Warenbezeichnungen usw. in
diesem Werk berechtigt auch ohne besondere Kennzeichnung nicht zu der Annahme,
dass solche Namen im Sinne der Warenzeichen- und Markenschutz-Gesetzgebung als frei
zu betrachten wären und daher von jedermann benutzt werden dürften.

Die Informationen in diesem Werk wurden mit Sorgfalt erarbeitet. Dennoch können
Fehler nicht vollständig ausgeschlossen werden und die Diplomica Verlag GmbH, die
Autoren oder Übersetzer übernehmen keine juristische Verantwortung oder irgendeine
Haftung für evtl. verbliebene fehlerhafte Angaben und deren Folgen.

Alle Rechte vorbehalten

© Anchor Academic Publishing, Imprint der Diplomica Verlag GmbH
Hermannstal 119k, 22119 Hamburg
http://www.diplomica-verlag.de, Hamburg 2016
Printed in Germany

Assessing the Role of Globalisation in the Rise of New Right Attitudes in Germany and Italy

Abstract

This research examines the role of the various processes entailed in globalisation in the rise of the New Right in Italy and Germany. The first section aims to clarify what is meant by the term globalisation, for it is more easily used than defined. Thus, several perspectives, such as those of the tranformationalists and the hyperglobalists, are taken into account. Then, economic and cultural globalisation, considered to be the most influential forms of globalisation, are analysed in depth. The second part specifically examines the Italian and the German cases by analysing the political and ideological discourse of successful New Right cultural movements and parties, such as the Italian Northern League and National Alliance. This analysis explains the difference between the populist New Right and the extreme right, and how the rise of New Right parties can be linked with the strengthening of cultural and economic globalisation.

Content

Introduction	3
I. The Challenges in a World of Globalisation	6
1. Economic globalisation: Liberalisation	9
2. Cultural globalisation and national identity	13
II. Italy and Germany: New Right as Culture and Politics	18
1. New Right in Italy: *Lega Nord* and *Alleanza Nazionale*	18
2. *Lega Nord*: an illustrious European example of the ideology of the New Right	22
3. *Alleanza Nazionale*: between Old (extreme) and New Right	24
4. Germany's *Neue Rechte*: the emphasis on the *Volk*	27
5. *'Ostalgia'* in East Germany	30
Conclusion	35

Introduction

According to Kaldor in the current era a number of different political ideologies, such as cosmopolitanism, Europeanism, Islamic fundamentalism, capitalism, and nationalism are in competition.[1] Some of them are progressive and in favour of an increasingly globalised world, while others are nostalgic, 'backward-looking', and reject most of the current developments occurring that are inevitably transforming societies around the globe. The outcome of this competition between the various ideologies will determine the future of the international panorama.[2] One of the ideologies mentioned on which I will focus my attention in this paper is nationalism, or more specifically neo-nationalism, which can be defined as "nationalism in a globalised world of aggressive postcolonial and post-Cold War readjustment."[3] This paper will try to provide answers to questions such as whether neo- nationalism, which has often been considered out-of-date and as something of the past, is becoming a la mode again and whether it is being strengthened by the processes of globalisation. Indeed, the aim of this paper is to understand whether the New Right movements and nationalist populist parties in Western Europe, which base their entire political and ideological discourse on nationalism, have been growing stronger in the last two decades as a result of some of the developments the processes of globalisation entails (migration, free trade, cultural interconnectedness, political transnationalism, and Americanisation). These developments are pivotal in enhancing nationalistic sentiments, which often lead to xenophobic attitudes. To many, the future appears unpredictable, if not frightening, due to the 'newness' brought by the various processes of globalisation, which has transformed lifestyles as well as the economic and social contexts, often generating not happiness but misery. For many observers "the only true opponents of globalisation are the nationalists, who already for years denounce the ongoing process that has led to globalisation being a fact today."[4] As Hans-Georg Betz has tried to demonstrate, New Right populist parties have attracted "a sizeable portion of the Western European population; their deputies and

---

[1] Kaldor M., 'Nationalism and Globalisation', Nations and Nationalism Vol. 10 (1/2), 2004 p 162
[2] Ibid
[3] Gingrich A. 'Neo-nationalism and the reconfiguration of Europe' Social Anthropology Vo. 14 No. 2 2006 p 200
[4] CMtG (n.d) Nationalisten tegen Globalisering, available at: http://www.strijd.be/platform.htm Accessed on 10/01/08

representatives sit in local, regional, national, and European Parliaments, their leaders appeared as guest shows."[5] This paper will attempt to explain how it is possible that, sixty-three years after the terrible atrocities of the Second World War, the radical right has managed to regain popularity and to play an important role in the Europe of the 21st century. Radical right and extremist movements in general are not new to post-war Europe, yet the current wave of new right populist attitudes is not sporadic as it was in the past. Instead, it represents a transnational phenomenon that involves several Western European countries, such as Italy and Germany. This paper will take a similar view to 'the Contemporary Europe Research Centre's' (CERC) argument that "both globalisation and national populism are undoubtedly significant phenomena in the European politics of the 21st century" and that "globalisation is one of the main causes of the recent rise of national populism in Europe.''[6] In addition, national populist parties are often not seen as anti-globalisation movements, which are traditionally associated with left wing and anti fascist groups that have demonstrated against the meetings of 'institutions of globalisation' (e.g. G8 meetings) in various cities including Prague, Genoa, Seattle, and Gothenburg. Nevertheless, the national populist parties in the European Parliament have been the most successful opponents of globalisation, even though the term itself is often not used in their party programs.

Italy and Germany have been chosen as case studies for various reasons. First, they are both prominent members of the European Union, which has often been described as a perfect example of political and economic cooperation, as well as of cultural openness and interconnectedness. The EU has always been seen as an institution that advances notions of a cosmopolitan international community. At the same time, however, support for national populist parties appears to have increased in both countries. In Italy, for example, Umberto Bossi's anti-globalisation and anti-immigration Northern League Party has won the recent national elections by joining Berlusconi's conservative coalition, and has established a new own record by winning almost 10 per cent of the total votes. In Germany, if on the one hand the main New Right political party, the Republikaner, has not had any relevant influence, on the other the New Right cultural movement has increase in popularity and has attracted a

---

[5] Betz Hans-Georg, 'Radical Right-Wing Populism in Western Europe' (London: The Macmillan Press, 1994) p (preface)
[6] Mudde Cas 'Globalisation: The Multi-Faced Enemy?' <u>CERC Working Papers Series</u> No. 3/ 2004 p 1

sizeable portion not only of the population but also of prominent politicians, academics, and journalist from the more moderate centre-right. The second reason why Germany and Italy have been chosen is that the constitutions in both countries are strongly antifascist as they were constituted on the ashes of the respective fascist regimes (Germany and Italy have constitutions provisions which forbid attempts to reconstitute fascist parties), so until recently, nationalism and everything related to it was often considered a taboo, and radical right parties were always obscured. Most observers and political analysts believed that the military defeat of Hitler's Germany and Mussolini's Italy had put an end to the radical right movements, political parties, and ideologies in general. Even though essential differences remain between the fascist parties in the inter-war period and the recent rise of New Right parties since the latter "do not ideologically oppose liberal democracies"[7], however they do share similar views in regards to the importance of the nation and the homogeneity of the people.

The first part of this paper will attempt to define globalisation, since it is more easily used than defined, and analyse its most important features in order to understand how these can affect society as a whole and how these can give rise to nationalistic attitudes. By doing so, this paper will try to justify the argument that even though there are numerous factors to take into account when observing the rise of New Right attitudes and sentiments, the various processes of globalisation play a fundamental part in motivating citizens to turn to the radical right. The second part of this paper will focus specifically on the Italian and the German case by explaining the political and ideological discourse of both the New Right parties, such as the Italian Northern League and National Alliance, and cultural movements in order to comprehend why they are the primary opposers of a globalising world. Thus, this part will look at globalisation and its relation to notions such as nationalism, xenophobia, and 'welfare chauvinism.' The final section of the examination will briefly look at the rise of the New Right in other Western European countries such as France, concluding that it is more widespread than is believed and that globalisation, together with other factors, is one of the leading causes of this rise.

---

[7] Zaslove A. 'The Dark Side of European Politics: Unmasking the Radical Right' Journal of European Integration Vo. 26 No. 1 March 2004 p 63

Chapter I - The Challenges in a World of Globalisation

Since the end of the Cold War the term globalisation has been used repeatedly by politicians, journalists, academics, managers, and bankers across the world. It has become a buzzword that some use to describe everything that is happening in the world today. Globalisation is regarded by many as one of the greatest challenges facing humankind today. The former first Director-General of the World Trade Organisation (WTO), Renato Ruggiero, once stated that globalisation is a reality "which overwhelms all others"[8] and the former Secretary-General of the United Nations pointed out how "arguing against globalization is like arguing against the laws of gravity."[9] In the aftermath of 9/11 and the consequent 'war on terror' carried out in Afghanistan and Iraq, there have been several disputes over whether the era of globalisation is over or not. On the one hand, we find intellectuals such as J.R. Saul and Justin Rosenberg who believe in the 'collapse of globalism'[10] and that 'the age of globalisation is unexpectedly over'[11]. On the other hand, political analysts Steve Smith and John Baylis observe how the events of 11 September 2001 "probably more than any other single event, brought home just how globalised is the contemporary world"[12] and how the wars in Afghanistan and Iraq "have been further clear examples of what it means to call the current era a globalised one." Moreover, globalisation has been a matter of dispute between hyperglobalists and ultra-sceptics that have opposing views regarding the extent of its development. Globalists, including economists Friedman and Ohmae, argue that globalisation is the most important reality in contemporary history as it marks the beginning of a new era "characterised by the inevitable and positive consequence of the worldwide triumph of free market capitalism and Western liberalism."[13] Sceptics such as Hirst and Thompson, on the other hand, dismiss its significance arguing that there is no empirical evidence regarding the worldwide impact of globalisation and that by comparison with the

---

[8] WTO-2 (1996b) 'Ruggiero Calls for Trading System to be Kept in Line with Globalization Process'. WTO press release, 22 February
[9] "'Diplomacy can be effective', says Secretary-General Interview," UN Chronicle, Spring, 1998
[10] Saul, J. R. 'The Collapse of Globalism', (2005, London: Atlantic Books)
[11] Rosenberg, J. 'Globalization theory: a post-mortem', International Politics Vol. 42 (2), 2005 p 2
[12] Baylis J. & Smith S. 'The Globalization of World Politics', (2005, Oxford: Oxford University Press) p 1
[13] Pick D. 'The reflexive modernization of Australian Universities' Globalisation, Societies and Education, Vol. 2 , No 1, March 2004 p 5

period 1870 to 1914 the world is much less globalised economically, politically, and culturally.[14] Between these two extremes, a more cautious approach has been taken by transformationalists like Anthony Mcgrew, who regard globalisation as an important trend which coexists with other major developments and has a differentiated impact upon individual states. The transformationalists' view that "although there exist important continuities with previous phases of globalization, contemporary patterns of globalization constitute a distinctive historical form which itself is a product of a unique conjuncture of social, political, economic and technological forces,"[15] is perhaps the most objective and accurate one.

Globalisation is a slippery, contested, and heavily loaded concept so it is not surprising that it initiates intense debates. In normative terms, globalisation has been linked by some with 'progress, peace, and prosperity;' for others, it is synonymous with 'deprivation, disaster, and doom.'[16] But how do we define globalisation in descriptive terms? A peasant activist in Thailand once exclaimed that "we don't know what globalization is, but we have to act!"[17] These words perfectly symbolise the confusion, uncertainty, and contradiction surrounding the debate on globalisation, demonstrating how "it is impossible to avoid the issue, but difficult to specify what it involves."[18] To start with, globalisation can simply be considered a historical process characterised by the "widening, deepening, speeding up and growing impact of worldwide interconnectedness."[19] In fact, a globalised world is one in which "political, economic, cultural, and social events become more and more interconnected, and also one in which they have more impact."[20] This increased global interconnectedness of the world has initiated a process of 'time-space compression', caused by various factors, which will be briefly examined.

Firstly, the world has been 'shrinking' due to the "'stretching' of social, political, and economic activity across the political frontiers so that events, decisions, and activities

---

[14] Hirst P. & Thompson G. 'Globalization in Question: The International Economy and the Possibilities of Governance' (1999, Cambridge: Polity Press)
[15] Held D., Mcgrew A., Goldblatt D., and Perraton J., 'Global Transformations' (1999, Cambridge: Polity Press) p 429
[16] Scholte J. A. 'Globalization: a critical introduction' (2005, London: Palgrave Macmillan) p 14
[17] Ibid p 1
[18] Ibid
[19] Mcgrew A., 'Globalization and global politics' in Baylis J. & Smith S p 19
[20] Baylis J. & Smith S p 8

in one region of the world come to have significance for individuals and communities in distant regions of the globe."[21] Moreover, the growing "extensity, intensity and velocity of global interactions is associated with a deepening enmeshment of the local and global in so far as local events may come to have profound global consequences and global events can have serious local consequences, creating a growing collective awareness or consciousness of the world as a shared social space, that is, globality."[22] For example, the recent mortgage crisis in the USA has affected the worldwide economies by causing the world's largest banks to lose billions of dollars, giving rise to panic, disorientation, and instability on the world financial markets. Another example are the various civil wars and conflicts occurring in instable regions like the Middle East (Iraq and Palestine) or sub-Saharan Africa(Darfur), which augment the number of asylum seekers and illegal immigrants flowing into more stable or developed countries.

Secondly, the intensification of worldwide interactions has been prompted by its increased speed linked to the availability of modern and advanced technology. As David Held and Anthony McGrew have pointed out, globalisation is being intensified by the "accelerating pace of transborder interactions and processes as the evolution of worldwide systems of transport and communication increases the rapidity or velocity with which ideas, news, goods, information, capital and technology move around the world."[23] The invention of new systems of communication and transport, such as Internet, satellite television, mobile phones, e-mails, faxes, jet airplanes, and high-speed trains, have created a 'global village' by linking millions of individuals across the world.

Globalisation, however, is not only about an increased interaction between people. It is a process that affects us in very different ways. Today globalisation is being blamed for terrorism, global warming, unemployment, and numerous other factors. Some observers have asked themselves whether there is anything in the current era that is not caused by globalisation.[24] If on the one hand globalisation should be considered as an asymmetrical process as it has an unequal impact on different parts of the world,

---

[21] Held D. & McGrew A., 'Globalization/Anti-globalization' (2007, Cambridge: Polity Press) p 2
[22] Mcgrew A., 'Globalization and global politics' in Baylis J. & Smith S p 22
[23] Held D. & McGrew A., p 3
[24] Mudde C. p 3

however, on the other hand, it has significantly affected Europe, including Germany and Italy, in respect of economy, governance, and identity. More precisely, as political analysts such as Berger and Huntington have stressed, it would not be erroneous to speak of 'globalisations' since there are various dimensions of the process. The next section will examine the economic and the cultural dimensions, for they both have a notable influence on the rise of nationalist sentiments, which have benefited new right parties and organisations across Europe.

Economic globalisation: Liberalisation

Most analysts have focused on economic globalisation arguing that it is much more extensive than is cultural globalisation. While this point of view is without doubt questionable, it is safe to say that over the past thirty years "the network of trading relations, the globalisation of production (in particular, multinational corporations) and the growth of foreign direct investment (FDI) have grown at unprecedented levels." [25] Today, economic globalisation has developed on a historically unprecedented scale as national economies are currently much more enmeshed in global systems of production and trade than in any other preceding epoch. More and more states are vulnerable to the volatility of global financial markets and, therefore, "markets have become globalised to the extent that the domestic economy constantly has to adapt to global competitive conditions."[26] Furthermore, there has been a general reduction if not abolition of capital controls, foreign-exchange restrictions, and regulatory trade barriers, which has attempted to create an open and borderless world economy.[27] Globalisation has made it possible for capitalism to become more widespread and durable more than ever before, strengthening its position which has become prevailing in the world structure of production. According to Scholte, globalisation has played a major role in the advent of 'hypercapitalism': "the expansion of commodification and the greater organisational efficiency of

---

[25] Graziano P., 'Europeanization or Globalization?', Global Social Policy, Vol 3 (2) Sage Pubblications p 174
[26] Held D. & McGrew A p 110-111
[27] Scholte J. A. P 16

accumulation have created a situation that can suitably be termed hypercapitalist."[28] Moreover, the 'technological revolution' in transport and communication mentioned before has changed the ways in which surplus accumulation occurs: "globalisation has brought a new world division of labour, a rise of regionalism, greater concentration of production in giant corporations, more accumulation through consumerism and finance capital, and a move from a Fordist to post-Fordist regimes for the control of labour."[29]

Hence, it is not surprising that the intensification of transactions and organisational connections crossing national boundaries is considered by most observers as 'the cornerstone of globalization.'[30] This intensified development of economic transnational relations has undermined the role of the state in a significant manner. In this respect, Susan Strange has pointed out how state authority "has leaked away, upwards, sidewards, and downwards" and sometimes "just evaporated,"[31] while analysts such as Camilleri, Dunn, Ohmae, Baumann, and Schmidt consider globalisation the main responsible for the 'crisis' of the nation-state. Norman Lamont, a former British Chancellor of the Exchequer, once said that due the conditions of globalisation, "politicians and governments too often give the appearance of being in office without being in power."[32] Globalisation is certainly not the sole reason for the overshadowing of the state and it has not threatened the existence of the state, but it does have a huge impact. In a globalising world, sovereignty has attained a different meaning, with governance shifting away form the traditional Westphalian system and moving towards a 'multilevel' form of governance.

This rise of supraterritoriality has often triggered nationalist reactions. Many nationalist critics argue that priority must be given to the re-establishment of self-determination of the nation-states by separating them from global economic activities, reason being that a globalised economy has calamitous consequences such as uncontrollable fluctuations in foreign exchange rates, stock prices and other financial

---

[28] Ibid p 158
[29] Ibid p 23
[30] Evans Peter 'The Eclipse of the Sate?Reflections on Stateness in an Era of Globalization' World Politics Vol. 5.1 (1997) p 3
[31] Strange S. 'The Defective State' Daedalus Vol.124 (Spring 1995) p 56
[32] Assinder Nick 'Is Cameron the real power?' BBC News website 4 February 2008 Accessed on 10/03/08

values that can instantaneously devastate lives.[33] Europe must in fact be rebuilt around "solidly reinvigorated national states that cooperate defensively against the evil and dangerous consequences of globalisation"[34], which is by its very nature extremely unsafe, unsustainable, and unacceptable and has negative consequences. National populist, who believe in economic nationalism and 'welfare chauvinism': 'the economy should serve the nation and should be controlled by it, while a welfare state is supported, but only of the own people.'[35] Hence, they consider it harmful for national interests, primarily because a "global market means that foreigners could influence the national economy"[36] and cause high rates of unemployment. Indeed, in a global economy in which capital, labour, production, markets, information and technology are structured supranationally, high rates of unemployment are affected by intense competition, which is "played out globally, not only by the multinational corporations, but also by small and medium-size enterprises that connect directly or indirectly to the world market through their linkages in the networks that relate them to larger firms."[37] This causes individual governments to lose their ability to control national economies, but it also severely affects the work force.

Unemployment has grown rapidly in Europe and elsewhere as numerous companies 'relocate and downsize' in order to compete globally. Full employment has more often than not become unrealisable with some analysts, including Aronowitz, DiFazio, and Rifkin, foreseeing a 'jobless future' and 'the end of work'.[38] Many Europeans worry about losing their jobs due to the new economic world order and the global competition from Asia, Latina America, and the U.S, but also from internal competition as a consequence of the EU enlargement. Helle C. Dale found out that "the private sector in Europe has almost stopped producing new jobs since the 1970s, and twenty million Europeans are unemployed."[39] According to a recent poll undertaken by GfK, a German market research firm, in Italy over thirty eight percent

---

[33] Scholte p 16
[34] Gingrich A. 2006 p 200
[35] Muddle C. p 5
[36] Ibid p 6
[37] Castells M., 'The Informational Economy in the New International Division of Labor' in Carnoy M., Castells M., Cohen S.S. and Cardoso F.H. 'The New Global Economy in the Information Age' (1993, University Park: The Pennsylvania State University Press) p 19
[38] Scholte J. A. P p 32
[39] Dale H. C., 'Challenges Facing Europe in a World of Globalization', Heritage Lecture # 914, The Heritage Foundation, November 28, 2005 p1

of respondents felt that unemployment was the most pressing problem, while in Germany over eighty percent suffered the same anxiety.[40] Germany and Italy, both at the heart of the Euro zone, are "stagnating economically and yet seem unable to come to grips with the liberising changes needed in a world of globalization, competitive labour markets, and the mobile capital demands of our economies."[41]

These figures indicate that the process of economic globalisation, which has played a fundamental role in transforming Western democratic societies with the transition from a modern industrialised to a post-industrial form of capitalism, has left many European citizens in a precarious condition. A substantial part of the population is incapable of coping with the acceleration of economic, social, and, as the next section of this examination will illustrate, cultural modernisation. As Ralf Dahrendorf has pointed out, many people are threatened to become useless ("those whom the full citizens of society do not need") since they do not have the skills required in a modern and globalised economy.[42] Analysts such as Reich even speak of "high-tech elites ruling a jobless nation," arguing that in the current era, characterised by the shift from mass production to a specialised production, from the industrial sector to the service and information sector, and from mass consumption to 'specialised consumption,' the number of unemployed has reached unprecedented levels.[43] Paul Kennedy has highlighted other shifts in the economic sphere, linked to economic globalisation, which have increased uncertainty: "the rise of unaccountable global corporations and unregulated and uncontrollable financial markets; the ability of corporate interests…to impose their own changing grids of multifaceted activities regardless of national borders onto certain world regions; the pressures and worldwide insecurities associated with growing economic rivalry between industrial nations."[44] Those who find themselves in a precarious condition, often labelled as the 'losers of globalisation', often pin their hopes on radical right parties, which manage to attract a sizeable portion of the less advantaged through their populist slogans. Holmes illustrated how in a globalised economy 'fast-capitalism' results in the growth of job

---

[40] GfK Press release, 'Anxiety about unemployment, concerns about inflation and fear of crime', Findings of the GfK survey, Challenges of Europe 2005 p 1-3
[41] Dale H. C. p 1
[42] Cited in Schmitter H., 'A Comparative Perspective on the Underclass', Theory and Society Vo. 20 1991 p 460
[43] Ibid
[44] Kennedy P. & Danks C.J. 'Globalization and National Identities' (2001, London: Palgrave) p 7

insecurity which then leads to the drastic decline of the support for established left and right mainstream parties across Europe: "neo-nationalisms in Europe are directly related to, and have to be analysed in relation to, all central developments of a globalised fast-capitalism."[45]

This declining economy security in Europe as a result of globalisation has also increasingly encouraged the growth of racial intolerance in society at large. To paraphrase Wrench and Solomos "the current increase in racism, and the changes in its form and character, are closely linked to the process of rapid economic, social and political change affecting the population of western European countries."[46] In fact, as Stephen Castles points out, "The increased salience of racism.... reflects the rapid change in living and working conditions, the dissolution of the cultural forms and organisational structures of the working class, and the weakness and ambivalence of the state."[47]

Cultural globalisation and national identity

Another characteristic of globalisation that plays an important role in reviving nationalistic sentiments and New Right attitudes is its profound impact on national cultures and identities. Samuel Huntington has rightly pointed out how "cultural characteristics and differences are less mutable and hence less easily compromised and resolved than political and economic ones."[48] Moreover, Robert Lieber and Ruth Weisberg have rightly affirmed how "culture in its various forms now serves as a primary carrier of globalization…and constitutes an important arena of contestation for national, religious, and ethnic identity."[49] Paradoxically, globalisation has had equally a heterogenizing as well as a homogenizing effect on culture and identities,

---

[45] Holmes quoted in Gingrich A. 'Neo-nationalism and the reconfiguration of Europe' Social Anthropology Vo. 14 No. 2 2006 p 199
[46] Solomos J. & Wrench J. 'Race and Migration in Western Europe' (1993 Oxford: Berg Publishers Ltd) p 5
[47] Castles S. in Solomos & Wrench p 27
[48] Huntington S., 'The Clash of Civilizations?' Foreign Affairs, Vol. 72, No 3 Summer 1973 p 27
[49] Lieber R. J. & Weisberg R. E., 'Globalization, Culture, and Identities in Crisis' , International Journal of Politics, Culture and Society, Vol. 16 No. 2, Winter 2002 p 273

provoking on the one side a rejection towards the upsurge of multiple identities and the hybridisation of cultures due to migration, while at the same time there has been a clear condemnation of the universalisation of culture (or, as many commentators have defined it, a 'cultural synchronisation'[50]) due to the spread of American values, lifestyle, and language.

Globalisation has often been viewed by many as the means to enhance and consolidate the hegemonic position of the United States in the international arena as well as a way for spreading capitalism and neo-liberal policies. However, globalisation has also been used as a term to describe the preponderance of American mass culture, where American music, movies, clothing, fast food ('The imperialism of McDonald's') and sports have become predominant. In fact, according to Charles Krauthammer, columnist for the Washington Post, the US dominates "every field of human endeavour from fashion to film to finance. We (Americans) rule the world culturally, economically, diplomatically and militarily as no one has since the Roman Empire."[51] It is therefore not surprising that Anti-Americanism has grown since the end of the Cold War in the early 1990s and that globalisation, perceived as the emblem of American economic, military, and cultural primacy, and therefore, synonymous to the Americanization of society, has helped forge neo nationalist sentiments in Europe and elsewhere. According to Pew Survey, critical assessments of American-style democracy and capitalism in countries such as Germany and Italy are far more extensive than in the developing nations of the Third World.[52] The words of Karsten Voight, a German former foreign ministry official of the Social Democratic Party, are helpful to understand the influence of American culture:

"The USA has long been setting standards on a worldwide basis, not just for the general populace, but has been leading the field in the classic cultural spheres, for example in research and teaching, or film and modern art. Its global role is rooted in a hitherto unknown blend of economic power, the ability to set the global cultural agenda and military superiority."[53]

---

[50] Warnier J. P. 'La mondialisation de la culture' [The Globalisation of Culture] (2003 Paris : Edition la Decouverte') p 1
[51] Krauthammer C., 'Who Needs Gold Medals' Washington Post, February 20, 2002
[52] Pew Global Attitudes Project, 'What the World thinks in 2002,' p 2
[53] Voight Karsten, speaking in Washington on March 8,2002, quoted in Rodman P., 'Uneasy Giant:The Challenges to American Predominance' (Washington DC, The Nixon Center, June 2002) p 1

An example of the influence of American culture is the spread of the English language in the world, which has become widely used and has become the international 'lingua franca'. Language has a key role in forging national feeling or cultural dignity and identity.[54] English is the predominant language of both the European Union and the United Nations, where over 120 countries correspond, and more than 85 percent of international organisations use it as one of their official languages.[55] Another cultural sphere in which there is a strong American influence is entertainment. Hollywood films have a market share of more than 70 percent in the Western countries, and as much as 90 per cent in other parts of the world.[56] The U.S market share of the cinema audience ranges from the 60 per cent in Italy to the 76 per cent in Germany.[57] In fact, in Berlin, following the opening of the Sony Centre (a colossal business and entertainment complex), a multiplex cinema centred there featured Hollywood films on eight of its nine screens.[58] Culture is therefore the most noticeable realm and this strong influence is the reflection of the increasing 'soft power' of the US, which indirectly affects the behaviour and interests of global consumers. The most natural reaction to this American predominance is to revive and reassert one's identity and national culture. It is therefore not unexpected that New Right movements and parties, which base their entire ideology on the uniqueness of a nation's identity and culture and fiercely oppose any form of Americanisation of society, are viewed by many as the only credible actors capable of revitalising one's identity. The view of the New Right in this respect is best summarised by the words of Louis Hebron and John Stack, which describe the Americanisation of society as "this foreign invasion and assimilation of cosmopolitan consumerism with a materialistic orientation, indulgent values, moral bankruptcy and fraternizing of nationalities [that] is a prescription of cultural genocide because of the process' potential to vulgarize and destroy the rich diversity of human civilisations."[59]

---

[54] Stergios J. 'Language and Nationalism in Italy' Nations and Nationalism Vol 12 (1) 2006 p 19
[55] 'A World Empire By Other Means', The Economist (London), December 22 2001, p 65-67
[56] 'Globalization and Cinema : An International Review of Culture and Society' The Committee on Intellectual Correspondance, Council on Foreign Relations, No. 8 Summer/Fall 2001 p 1
[57] Data from 'US Market Share of Film Industry for Select Countries' Global Policy Forum www.globalpolicy.org Accessed on 17/03/08
[58] Lieber R. J. & Weisberg R. E., 'Globalization, Culture, and Identities in Crisis', International Journal of Politics, Culture and Society, Vol. 16 No. 2, Winter 2002 p 279
[59] Hebron L. & Stack J. F. 'The Globalization Process: Debunking the Myths.' Paper presented at the annual meeting of the International Studies Association, Chicago, 20-24 February 2001

The heterogenization of cultures and identities, however, has had a much bigger impact in reinforcing nationalistic sentiments. Global connectivity has increased contact with the foreigner, consequently raising the awareness of and determination to maintain national distinctiveness. For many Europeans 'foreign' has become a synonym for danger.[60] The new patterns of migration and settlement promoted by the process of globalisation have in fact significantly affected Europe as the number of migrants settling in Western European countries has raised significantly. Indeed, in Western Europe xenophobia and racism started to emerge and to reach unprecedented levels in the early 1990s when, due to the process of modernisation, economic globalisation, and the consolidation of capitalism, Western European countries attracted thousands of immigrant workers from the Third World. During the 1970s and the 1980s, a great majority of the immigrant population came form other European countries, whereas from the beginning of the 1990s the vast majority of the immigrant workforce was from non EU countries. According to Eurispes, a major Italian research institute, already in 1991 the vast majority of immigrants came from the non-EU countries (the so-called *exrtacommunitari*): over thirty per cent came form Africa, mostly from the Maghreb region, twenty six per cent was from Asia and Latin America, and less than twenty five per cent was from the European Union.[61] This rapid transformation led to a strong anxiety among Western Europeans who feared that "some fundamental, unexpected and irrevocable changes have taken place because of recent large scale immigration" that threaten "the historically given self-perceptions of European nations."[62] This has lead to the emergence of a vigorous debate about the rise of a multicultural society and whether or not Western European societies should attempt to integrate immigrants without obliging them to abandon their traditions and cultures. In Germany, the Allesbacher Berichte found out that only 23 per cent of the population viewed multiculturalism in a positive way, many of which stated that foreigners constitute a threat to the German identity and way of life[63]. In addition, a large minority believed that 'Volkervermischung' (mixing of

---

[60] Rothkop D. 'In praise of Cultural Imperialism? Effects of Globalization on Culture' Foreign Policy June 22, 1997 p 1
[61] 'Rapporto Italia 91' EURISPES 1991 (Rome: Vallecchi Editore)
[62] Hammar T. 'Comparing European and North American International Migration', International Migration Review Vo. 23 No. 3 1989 p 637
[63] Multikulturelle Gesellschaft', Allesbacher Berichte No. 9 1992

peoples) should be avoided in order to keep the German people 'pure'.[64] The Human Development Report of the United Nations shows how people who fear that the continuous arrival of immigrants, mostly from the developing world, constitutes a serious threat to the national values of a country, make three arguments: "that immigrants do not assimilate but reject the core values of the country; that immigrant and local cultures clash, inevitably leading to social conflict and fragmentation; and that immigrant cultures are inferior and if allowed a foothold would undermine democracy and retard progress, a drain on economic and social development."[65] Moreover, these words reflect a growing concern that in the long run the foreign population might overtake and decrease the indigenous Western European population due to its high birth rates, leading the latter into a minority status.

In sum, the explanation for this increased hostility towards immigrants in Western Europe is best to be found in the anxiety and resentment which has appeared and developed due to the numerous uncertainties caused by the social, economic, and cultural transformation of advanced Western democracies in an era of globalisation, in which foreign presence is one of its most visible pieces of evidence. Slogans such as 'Auslander raus' and 'fuori gli immigrati' are "not isolated calls of a miniscule majority on the lunatic fringes of post-industrial Europe" but rather "express and reflect the attitudes and opinions of a sizeable portion of the core of West Europe's public."[66]

---

[64] Ibid
[65] 'Globalization and Cultural Choice' Human Development Report 2004 Ch. 5 p 100
[66] Betz Hans-Georg, 'Radical Right-Wing Populism in Western Europe' (London: The Macmillan Press, 1994) pp 96-97

Chapter II - Italy and Germany: New Right as Culture and Politics

New Right in Italy: *Lega Nord* and *Alleanza Nazionale*

As we have seen the various aspects and dimensions of globalisation have had a huge impact on the economics, politics, and culture of nation states. The intensification of worldwide interactions prompted by its increased speed linked to the availability of modern technology, the advent of 'hypercapitalism,' global financial markets, and its global competitive conditions, the rise of supraterritoriality and the weakening of the tradition Westphalian political system, the Americanisation of national cultures, and the constant rise of immigration influx have all affected people's lives. Italian sociologist Umberto Melotti has defined the process of globalisation affecting his country as 'the ultimate act of a drama' due to:

"the formation and extension of the capitalist system to a global scale, with all its contradictions. Beyond that it represents the first chapter in a new stage in history. This stage is characterised by the transformation of the world into a new configuration of multiracial, multiethnic, multicultural, multilinguistic, and multi-religious social formations. These new social formations are divided by increasing diversity, and yet also more independent, and thus at least tendentially united in their destiny."[67]

Especially since the early 1990s, these numerous and fast growing transformations described by Melotti have caught many citizens unprepared and have caused many of them to be concerned about the future of both their jobs and identities. Many northern Italians, especially workers and less educated, are preoccupied about the impact of globalisation on their economic well-being. In a survey conducted by Ludovico Gardani, over 58 per cent of respondents said that external political developments affected their regions and almost 70 per cent believed that global economic developments in Europe and the world directly affected their region. In Lombardy, the

---

[67] Melotti U 'L'immigrazione straniera in Italia;dati, cause, tipi'' Inchiesta 20 (October/December) p 170

percentage was extremely high; nearly 80 per cent of those interviewed claimed that the region was influenced by world dynamics.[68] Gardani analysed his survey and concluded that "globalisation creates a sense of uncertainty and anxiety, pushing individuals, particularly those who do not have any first hand experience with global dynamics, toward territorial identification and support for enhanced local power."[69]

The recent elections in the country, in which the conservative PDL Party and its new right Northern League ally won the elections with a strong majority of votes, is one of the most evident symptoms of the fears and uncertainties that hang over the population. In fact, the recent Italian elections held on the 13th and 14th of April this year produced unexpected results, giving a significant majority to Silvio Berlusconi's 'People of Freedoms' (PDL) coalition, composed of the PDL Party itself, which was recently created by the merging of Berlusconi's Forza Italia Party and Gianfranco Fini's conservative National Alliance Party, and the anti-globalisation and anti-immigration Northern League Party. In the Senate, Berlusconi's centre-right coalition obtained 46.5 per cent of votes against the 37.54 per cent received by Walter Veltroni's centre left coalition (PD- Democratic Party).[70] In the Chamber of Deputies, the centre right coalition claimed 45 per cent of votes whereas the PD received only 48.1 per cent of total votes.[71] The most surprising aspect of this stunning victory however is that the Northern League Party strongly enhanced its usual performance, more than doubling its previous record, by claiming alone almost 9 per cent of the votes in the Senate and 6 per cent in the Chamber of Deputies. This allowed Umberto Bossi's new right party to obtain 60 seats in the Chamber of Deputies and 25 seats in the Senate.[72]

The extraordinary results of Bossi's Northern League Party are the most important political response of the electorate to the transformations of globalisation. Of course, globalisation and its consequences are not the sole reason of this huge success. The

---

[68] Beirich H. & Woods D. 'Globalisation, workers and the northern league' West European Politics Vo. 23 No. 1 p 140
[69] Ludovico Gardani quoted in Beirich H. & Woods D. 'Globalisation, workers and the northern league' West European Politics Vo. 23 No. 1 p 141
[70] Antonucci Germano 'People of Freedoms triumphs-Northern League doubles vote' Corriere Della Sera 15 April 2008, www.corriere.it Accessed on 15/04/08
[71] Ibid
[72] Ibid

countless failures of the previous centre-left coalition government headed by Romano Prodi consistently influenced the outcome of the elections. First and foremost, the Naples rubbish emergency, which has hit people's pocket, heightened anxiety about public health, and heavily damaged the country's image abroad, can be seen as the symbol of a broader crisis affecting Italy, which is 'blocked': its economy is fragile and underperforming; its politics are stagnant; and all attempts at reform have failed.[73] Another unresolved problem that has helped to bring down Romano Prodi's government is represented by Alitalia's crisis. The national airline has been losing around 1 million Euros a day, hampered by an aging, inefficient fleet, rising fuel costs and frequent labour strikes.[74] Moreover, Prodi's centre-left government has taken a lot of unpopular measures such as the soar tax increases it imposed.

Nevertheless, the changes brought by economic, political, and cultural globalisation had a primary role in shaping peoples political preferences because the central government has been seen as unable to cope with the socioeconomic and socio-cultural crisis of Italian society in a period of rapid modernisation. One of the most influential consequences of globalisation affecting the lives of Italian citizens considerably is immigration.

Before the 1990s, most Italians were either indifferent or showed minimal fear towards immigration, even though Italy started to move from a country of emigration to one of immigration in the beginning of the 1970s. The first immigrants came to Italy about forty years ago when the global recession, poverty and conflicts in the Third World, and the growing economy in Italy (the Italian economy became one of the most powerful global economies with its GDP exceeding that of Britain in the 1980s) contributed to a gradual increase in levels of immigration. Between 1981 and 1985, the foreign population in Italy grew by 7.2 percentage points, whereas between 1986 and 1990 it increased by 16.7 points. However, it was during the 1990s that levels of immigration rose dramatically reaching unprecedented figures. After the end of the Cold War and the collapse of the Soviet Union, the process of economic globalisation, which promoted liberalism and 'hypercapitalism', accelerated considerably. The technological revolution in transport and communication, the move

---

[73] 'Italy's election: Promises, but no delivery' The Economist, March 29th 2008 p 49-50
[74] 'Alitalia: Rapid Descent' The Economist, March 22nd 2008 p 84

from a Fordist to a post-Fordist regime, the growing economic and political interconnectedness which transformed the world in a 'global village,' all played an important role in intensifying and increasing patterns of migration in Italy, but also in Germany and elsewhere in Western Europe. The OECD report on Trends in International Migration claimed in fact that Italy was "the second-ranking receiving country after Germany, with inflows rising by over 20% in 1999."[75]

This partly explains why by the beginning of the 1990s, fear and anxiety about immigrants started to develop and social protests were backed not only by the poor and the underprivileged, but also by a wide-cross part of society including professionals and the middle class. Ilvo Diamanti, a prominent Italian political analyst, has conducted a comparative study confirming that today immigration has become a central issue in Italy. Diamanti found out that 42.8 per cent of Italians surveyed believed that immigration was a threat to public order and security (above the EU average of 31.9 per cent); 32.3 per cent felt that immigrants were a threat to job security (similar to the EU average of 33.2 per cent); finally, another 25 per cent (close to the EU average of 25 per cent) stated that immigration is a danger to culture and identity.[76] This study shows how those interviewed worry not only about losing their identity and culture, but also about the impact that immigration can have on issues like crime and security. Populist and new right parties like the Northern League and National Alliance took advantage of these fears and made use of 'scare tactics', typical of the populist language. For example, on an article published in 2000 on its official newspaper, La Padania, alarmist tones were used to predict that by 2010 Italy will have three million legal immigrants and that policemen would not be in a position to carry out their duties anymore.[77] Immigration is also used to exploit issues of employment: "immigrants take jobs, homes, and social services from local citizens, while they also lower the cost of labour while raising costs for an already overburdened welfare state."[78] Moreover, the current minister of Labour and central figure of the Lega Nord Roberto Maroni, affirmed that immigration forces down wages and therefore "foreigners must only be given work that citizens of each

---

[75] OECD, 'Trends in International Migration' (Geneva: OECD 2001) p 192
[76] Diamanti Ilvo, 'Immigrazione e Cittadinanza in Europa'', <u>Fondazione Nord Est</u>, February 2001 p 3
[77] 'Un altro milione di immigrati? Saranno un'ottima forza-lavoro,' <u>La Padania</u>, 21 June 2000
[78] Zaslove Andrej, 'The Dark Side of European Politics: Unmasking the Radical Right'', <u>Journal of European Integration</u> Vo. 26 (2004) p 23

community clearly do not want. The number will become set, based on the choice of the citizens. The fundamental concept is to prevent manpower from outside the EU from being used to the cost of labour."[79] This discourse attracts many workers who complain that immigrants "take their bread" and that immigration would be fine if "there were work for us." The logic behind this thinking is the following: "we are unemployed, they work, therefore they take our work....foreigners should not enjoy the opportunity to work in our country, even if we refuse the jobs they take, because they are undeserving in the sense that they have not contributed to it as we have."[80]

Experts on racism generally agree that Italians are not inherently racist, but that that the nation is finding it hard to absorb the recent arrival of developing-world migrants. According to the Evrigenis Report, "Italy is certainly one of the countries of Europe with the lowest number of racialist incidents" and Cavaterra confirmed this view by stating that Italy "is not a xenophobic country."[81] Nevertheless, several city authorities across Italy are clearing out gypsy settlements, blaming rising crime on a mass influx of migrants caused by both globalisation and European Union enlargement.

Lega Nord: an illustrious European example of the ideology of the New Right

Like many other radical right parties, the Northern League "employs an anti-bureaucratic, anti-elite, anti-European Union political message. This message is coupled with the scapegoating of immigrants and outsiders....and the opposing of economic and cultural globalisation."[82] The Lega Nord embraces and was instrumental in introducing in the Italian political context the ideology and philosophy of the French *La Nouvelle Droite,* which emphasizes the cultural differences between people. French intellectual Alain de Benoist, its most central figure, argues that "even

---

[79] Ibid p 1
[80] Cole J. 'The New Racism in Europe: A Sicilian ethnography' (1997, Cambridge: Cambridge University Press) p 67
[81] European Parliament, 'Report of The Committe of Inquiry Into Racism and Xenophobia', European Parliament Session Documents 23 July 1990 p 61
[82] Ibid p 25

though the human being is an animal, it is also more than just a biological entity; thus culture and history are essential for its survival."[83] Benoit claims that all cultures "have the inherent right to protect themselves from universalist, equalizing, homogenizing theories that attempt to assimilate or integrate all cultures into one body politic."[84] He insists on the right to protect one's culture: "each (cultural) universalism carries in itself a latent notion of racism, inasmuch as it places, as a universal value, the limitless projection of a particular system of values and norms."[85] Europeans have the obligation to protect the 'naturalness' and the 'purity' of their cultures from the homogenizing theories or theories of assimilation. Thus, Benoist and La Nouvelle Droite are firmly against multiculturalism and the mixing of different cultures brought by the process of globalisation because this leads to "discrimination, segregation, cultural decadence and delinquency."[86] Bossi's Northern League applies this 'right to difference' conceived by the Nouvelle Droite to direct the attention on the increasing numbers of immigrants in Italy and across Europe. In fact, the Lega Nord argues that citizens have the right and duty to defend themselves from universalism, homogenization, capitalism, multinational corporations, and the EU because these economic and political forces "push different cultures on each other against the will of the people."[87] In sum, multicultural and multiracial societies, that are encouraged and strengthened by the economic and political forces behind globalisation, threaten not only "the identity of the local, the North, Italy, and Europe," but also "local employment and competition for employment."[88]

Multiculturalism is seen as a product of globalisation and Americanization, whereas globalisation is viewed as a way of introducing and facilitating the supremacy of capitalism as well as the American consumer culture in all aspects of European social and cultural life. According to Bossi, "globalisation is linked to American society, American politics, American culture, and American interests and its desire to colonize Europe and the world with fast food, Hollywood, and music."[89] Moreover, if

---

[83] Benoist Alain, ' L'Equivoco del Razzismo: Per una critica differenzialista,' Transgressioni Vo. 7 (1988) p 22
[84] Zaslove A 'The Politics of Exclusion: Radical Right Populism and the Lega Nord' Paper presented at the Annual meeting of the American Political Science Association on Sep 01 2005 p 8
[85] Benoist Alain p 26
[86] Ibid p 29
[87] Zaslove A. p 12
[88] Ibid p 13
[89] Cited in Zaslove p 18

multiculturalism is the essence of American society, European society is instead characterized by a substantial historical and cultural homogeneity. The Northern League believes that the process of globalisation and Americanization of the European society must be strongly opposed in order to avoid the creation of a consumer culture and a multicultural society, which would lead to internal conflict and violence between different identities. As the Lega's provincial secretary of the province of Mantova affirmed, "multicultural societies do not work, have not worked, and cannot work"[90] and that globalisation must be opposed to avoid homogenization of society. Bossi argued how transforming Italy into a "multi-racial, multi-ethnic, and multi-religious country modeled after the US meant to keep Italy divided" and that "a multicultural society comes closer to hell than to paradise."[91] In sum, members of the Lega Nord loudly argue that "multiculturalism, globalisation (economic and cultural), and the Americanisation of society threatens the identity of the local....thereby eroding the cultural, spiritual, moral, and economic fabric of society."[92]

Alleanza Nazionale: between Old (extreme) and New Right

The National Alliance party, which has recently fused with Berlusconi's Forza Italia party to create the PDL party, has a historical and ideological legacy with Fascism. Indeed, *Alleanza Nazionale* stems from the former neo-fascist party MSI (Movimento Sociale Italiano), created in the post-war years. In the last decade AN has made an attempt to move away from the most extremist positions and its leader Gianfranco Fini has more times stated that his party was willing to join the European People's Party, the largest centre-right party on a European level.[93] The discourse of AN, however, is still nationalist and stresses the need to maintain values of national and ethnic identity, as well as the sovereignty of the citizens. AN also blames capitalism and economic globalisation for the rise of immigration and questions whether the Italian nation can remain intact if it is mixed with distinct cultures. According to a study conducted by Gianfranco Baldini and Rinaldo Vignati, almost 60 per cent of

---

[90] Ibid
[91] Bossi cited in Betz Hans-Georg p 122
[92] Ibid p 20
[93] 'Martens: "Impossibile An in Ppe", Fini: "Solo opinioni personali"', La Republica 22 November 2006

AN delegates agreed that a rise in the number of immigrants would damage national identity and 65 per cent believed that welfare benefits should be excluded to immigrants.[94] The party officially condemns racism, anti-Semitism and the anti-immigrant acts of skinheads, but it views immigration as a problem. AN representatives argue that it would be positive and beneficial for all those concerned if immigrants would return to their countries since each country should preserve its own culture and identity. In fact, AN ideology is characterized by ethnic nationalism: "The nation is not defined in political but in ethnic terms.....The state should be an expression of ethnic community and those who do not belong to this ethnic community are excluded from the nation."[95] This ideology refuses egalitarian values and argues in favour of 'inequality by nature'. Indeed, it praises ethnic autonomy and opposes both the 'egalitarian myth' and the dynamism and territorial mobility of globalisation, which have 'devastating effects'. AN delegates like Alberto Simeone believe that "the informal processes of economic globalisation are made responsible for the fact that authentic cultures have lost their roots" and, based on the New Right ideologies' typical assumption, argues that "diversity should not be destroyed as in Nazi-Fascist ideology, but positively valued."[96] This notion of 'their own identities' is centered on the assumption that each people has its own history, destiny and immutable identity, and these should not be mixed. Therefore, the identity of the Italian nation is diverse and cannot coexist with that of the immigrants, so there is the need to protect Italian identity against the influence of immigrants even though, as Roberto Menia admits, "movements of populations, emigration and immigration are phenomena connected to the development of the planet: they cannot be stopped, or avoided, nor is it possible to raise great Chinese walls."[97] Nevertheless, Maurizio Gasparri, former Minister of Communications and one of the top politicians of AN, points out how " we [of the National Alliance] are not ashamed to say that Italians come first; of course, the rights of all have to be guaranteed, but the Italian

---

[94] Baldini G. & Vignati R. 'Dal MSI ad AN: una nuova cultura politica?', Polis, Vo. 10 No. 1 (1996) p 83
[95] Fennema M., 'Some Theoretical Problems and Issues in Comparision of Anti-immigrant Parties in Western Europe', Working Paper no. 115 (Barcelona: Instituto de Ciencies Politiques I Socials 1996) p 9
[96] Ter Wal J. 'The Discourse of the Extreme Right and its Ideological Implications: The Case of the Alleanza Nazionale on Immigration' Patterns of Prejudice Vo. 34 No. 4, 1 October 2000 p 44
[97] Roberto Menia quoted in Ter Wal J. 'The Discourse of the Extreme Right and its Ideological Implications: The Case of the Alleanza Nazionale on Immigration' Patterns of Prejudice Vo. 34 No. 4, 1 October 2000 p p 45

government, the Italian parliament, has to guarantee the rights of Italians, of unemployed Italians, of those who see their own freedom threatened by illegal activities committed by indigenous Italians but sustained by immigrant manpower....We cannot promise everyone a paradise on earth."[98]

The anti-immigrant rhetoric of AN was evident when, after the wife of a prominent Italian Navy officer was raped and then killed by a Romanian of Roma origins in November of 2007, Gianfranco Fini and other members of the party called for mass repatriation and the closing of the country's frontiers. A few days after the arrest of the Romanian criminal for, Fini vehemently criticised Gypsies in general since they considered "theft to be virtually legitimate and not immoral" and felt the same way about "not working because it has to be the women who do so, often by prostituting themselves."[99] He also stated that Gypsies "had no scruples about kidnapping children or having children [of their own] for the purposes of begging" and concluded by saying that all the Roma camps in Italy should be torn down and 100,000 to 200,000 people expelled because "to talk of integration with people with a culture of that sort is pointless."

---

[98] Maurizio Gasparri quoted in Ter Wal J. 'The Discourse of the Extreme Right and its Ideological Implications: The Case of the Alleanza Nazionale on Immigration' Patterns of Prejudice Vo. 34 No. 4, 1 October 2000 p47

[99] Hooper J. 'Italian right calls for repatriation of Roma', The Guardian Monday November 5 2007

Germany's *Neue Rechte*: the emphasis on the *Volk*

The New Right in Germany has often been considered rather insignificant. Yet, since the 1990s the *Neue Rechte* has turned into an influential ideological network which has had a huge impact on the German public. The German New Right is not a homogenous movement and it does not have a single cohesive ideology. In fact, there is little agreement about what the New Right actually is. On the one hand, supporters of the New Right argue that it is a political and cultural movement that: rejects universalism, pluralism, cosmopolitanism, individualism, liberalism, parliamentarism, equality, and multiculturalism; stresses the importance of German nationalism and self-assertiveness; differs substantially from the Old Right and its National Socialist model.[100] Other commentators and observers like Pfahl-Traughber claim that, instead, there is no clear dividing line between the Old and New Right since they share the same ideology, tactic, propaganda, and seeks to delegitimise the democratic constitutional state.[101] The best definition seems to be provided by Minkenberg: the New Right in Germany provides "a crucial link between established conservatism and the openly anti-democratic extremists on the right by radicalising conservative positions on the on hand, and legitimizing right positions on the other."[102] The New Right lies, therefore, in the mainstream of political and cultural thought. Notorious New Right periodicals include Junge Freiheit, Nation und Europe, Europa Vorn, Wir Selbst, Staatbrief, Criticon, Deutsche Monatshefte. Many politicians of the mainstream conservative party (CDU) contribute to New Right publications: CDU members such as Axel Fisher, Jochen-Konrad Fromme, Klaus-Jurgen Hedrich, Rudriger Goldmann, and Heinrich Lummer have all written publications on the 'Junge Freiheit,' one of the most notorious German New Right magazines.[103] Politicians are not the only contributors since political analysts, historians, philosophers, and journalists from the conservative right constantly provide commentary for New Right newspapers and journals.

---

[100] Stoss R., Forschungs und Erklarungsansatze- ein Uberblick', in Recht
[101] Pfahl-Traughber A., ‚Rechtextremistische Intellektuelle gegen den demokratischen Verfassungsstaat' (1998, Opladen: Leske und Budrich) p 158-159
[102] Minkenberg M., 'German Unification and the Continuity of Discontinuities: Cultural Change and the Far Right in East and West', German Politics, Vol. 2 1994 p 178
[103] Woods R. p 18

The German New Right, similarly to the other mainstream European New Right parties and movements, rejects globalisation in general because it symbolises negative elements and values such as liberalism ('cancer of our century')[104] and the 'exclusive and repressive' capitalist system,[105] as well as the advent of an empty and insignificant materialist age, which lacks of meaning and purpose. According to the main New Right party, the Republikaner, which broke into the national German political scene in 1989, one of the biggest threats is posed by the process of globalisation in shaping and transforming the role of the nation. On the one hand, the nation state has become too small to tackle the 'big issues' and the world-scale threats.[106] Globalisation and liberalism are both seen as synonyms of materialistic nihilism, consumerism, world-weariness, the crisis of the soul, cosmopolitanism (defined as 'universal genocide')[107] and egalitarianism, which are all symbols of today's widespread decadence. According to the Republikaner, the best way to contrast the numerous negative effects of the globalising process in the 21st century is by placing "the nation at the centre of our thinking as an effective force, a historical fact that is at its best both fatherland and motherland, offering a community based on a shared destiny, language, culture, identity as well as a political framework for our actions and a cultural framework for our guidance."[108] Nationalism is therefore a key element because there is no alternative to the nation that can meet the needs of a community. The importance of placing the nation at the centre of our thinking is explained by Alfred Mechtersheimer, a prominent New Right thinker:

"National refers to the nation, that is to say to a community based on a political act of will by people who are laying claim not just to a shared identity but also to their right to be different. What a people have in common may be culture, language, religion or history; the nation manifests itself in a political consciousness of common values, intensions and a wish to prevail……it is clear that the nation satisfies in a particularly profound way the basic social need of people for a sense of belonging."[109]

---

[104] Brinks J.H, Rock S., Timms E., 'Nationalist Myths and Modern Media: Contested Identities in the Age of Identities' (2006, London:Tauris Academic Studies) p 131
[105] Grund C. J. 'Euro-Gesellschaft statt Volk', Nation und Europa, Vo. 46 December 1996 p 39
[106] Schroder R., 'Wie weit verbindet die Deutschen die gemeinsame Nation?', Wir Selbst, Vo. 3 No. 1999 p 12
[107] Krebs P. ,'Die europaische Wiedergeburt' (1982, Tubingen: Grabert) p 33
[108] Woods Roger (2007) p 96
[109] Mechtersheimer A. quoted in Woods Roger p 37-38

Culture is one of the cornerstones of the nations since it shapes the patterns of behaviour, offers 'common goals', and is a guide for the community. Culture is the foundation of German identity as it is ethnic, homogenous, and marks nations off each other. The differences between cultures are not inconsiderable and "cannot simply be shrugged off, because culture is man's second nature."[110] This emphasis on culture, the 'Volk' (the people) and the nation goes hand in hand with racist attitudes, even though it is not openly acknowledged. Since different cultures cannot coexist, immigration is regarded as a major external threat to German identity. 'Prussian values' (order, discipline, punctuality, a sense of duty, and physical toughness) are constantly threatened by the foreign population. Junge Freiheit insisted that even though there was an irreversible decline in the birthrate of the indigenous population, immigration was not the solution because "our cultural identity cannot take a wave of immigration, allowing people to pour in who in one way or another wish to change the world we live in.... our principles, our values."[111] Multiculturalism is viewed as a form of disintegration causing society to fall apart into a plurality of ways of life and Europeans ought to react to this danger by encouraging an ethnocultural homogeneity of the Europeans ('heterogeneous world of homogenous nations')[112] Brubaker explains how German nationhood "was conceived not as the bearer of universal political values, but as an organic cultural linguistic, or racial community; the nationhood is constituted by ethnocultural unity."[113] New Right thinkers tend to remind that even the constitution of the German Republic is based on the belief that the modern German state is "legitimacy founded on one culture and one nation."[114] Multiculturalism must therefore be prevented to achieve a 'Germany for the Germans.' Pierre Krebs and Rolf Stolz argue that the Turkish community in Germany, which is the country's largest ethnic minority with its 2.6 million units, is forming a 'state within a state.' Many Germans appear to share the same fear since in their cities with more than 200,000 residents, forty five per cent of children under the age of 16 have a migration background, which means that they are immigrants themselves or have parents or grandparents who immigrated into the country.[115] Across Germany

---

[110] Weismann Karlheinz quoted in Woods Roger pg37
[111] Wiesberg M. 'Der Westen muss sich wehren', Junge Freiheit, 6 September 2002
[112] Brinks J.H, Rock S., Timms E p 128
[113] Brubaker W.R. 'Citicenship and Nationhood in France and Germany' (1992, Cambridge, Mass: Harvard University Press) p 17
[114] Wrench & Solomos p 70
[115] 'Two unamalgamated worlds', The Economist April 5th 2008 p 31

itself, the proportion is of almost a third. There is a risk that this large ethnic minority might create 'parallel societies' unable to coexist with German culture and values. Turkey's prime minister, Recep Tayyip Erdogan, further exacerbated this widespread fear among the German population when, on a recent official visit to Germany last February, urged the Turkish community to hold itself detached from German society since "assimilation is a crime against humanity.....and Turkish children should be able to study in Turkish language schools and at a Turkish university." [116] Paradoxically, this view is very close to the New Right's philosophy of one Volk and Benoit's 'right to difference.' Many Turks living in Germany argue that the indigenous population does not facilitate the process of integration since however high they rise and however good their German is, they continue to be considered foreign. Indeed, according to a study conducted by Faruk Yen of the Centre for Studies on Turkey in Essen, over two-thirds of Turkish residents consider themselves as victims of discrimination.[117]

Ostalgia in East Germany

It is not surprising that support for the New Right discourse and ideology is superior in the eastern part of Germany than it is elsewhere. The former communist GDR (German Democratic Republic) had a difficult time in trying to adapt to and confront the new challenges of globalisation. Unification dramatically increased Germany's economic and social problem. The difficulties for West Germany arose when West Germans "exported their high wages, generous benefits, and stifling regulations to the east-just when this brand of capitalism was beginning to flag under global competition."[118] In Eastern Germany, however, the consequences of unification were more problematic. The collapse of the socialist state and the monumental task of reunification have exposed the GDR to the pressures and changes of a globalising world. The economic and social concerns became overwhelming with the sudden rise of the proportion of foreigners (before 1990, the number of resident immigrants in the GDR was negligible), which led to strained public attitudes towards immigrants.

---

[116] Ibid
[117] Ibid p 32
[118] 'Germany: Is Reunification Failing?' <u>Business Week</u>, November 15 1993 p 49

There was a sense of overcrowding and deprivation that was much higher in the east: during the 1990s, unemployment rose to almost 40 per cent, and 50 per cent of the Ostdeutschen had xenophobic sentiments compared to the 30 per cent of westerns. These high levels of xenophobia in Eastern Germany can be considered as "an indication of identity confusion in the face of globalizing cross-pressures".[119] Indeed, the Ostdeutschen, which still had to get used to the new 'multi-German identity', were at the same time challenged by the advancement of a multi-ethnic and multi-cultural society. In addition, the process of globalisation introduced a materialist and postmodernist culture, which was in stark contrast with the eastern German community's prior patterns and experience of "limited supplies and suppressed consumer demands."[120] Boyes showed how East Germans are "not hugely impressed by the reality of life under global capitalism", since unemployment and insecurity seem to be generating a German 'mezzogiorno'.[121]

Many Eastern Germans seem to find that the German Volk has lost its character due to the Americanised mentality. Before unification, Germany has always been regarded as the most pro-American Western European nation. American practices, norms, and culture have had a crucial role in shaping Germany's economy, society, culture, and politics. Now Americanisation, defined as the "adoption of American forms of production and consumption, technology and techniques of management, cultural goods and institutions of mass culture, gender roles, and leisure practices"[122] is being opposed due to resentment and fear of modernity, mass culture. Moreover, there is a different perspective on capitalism and the 'rules of the economic life': "in America, money is the goal and things are the means to achieve it, while in Germany our goal is to achieve things, with money as the means."[123] The Republikaner criticise American hypercapitalism accusing it to be endorsing the global mobility of labor in order to achieve higher profits which has led to the standardisation of consumer products, the way of life, and ultimately the Volk. Franz Schonhuber, one of the founders of Die

---

[119] Hogwood P. 'Identity in the former GDR: Expressions of Ostalgia and Ossi pride in United Germany' in Kennedy P. & Danks C. J. 'Globalization and National Identities: Crisis or Opportunity?' (2001, London: Palgrave) p 66

[120] Ibid p 76
[121] Boyle quoted in Sweeney Simon 2005 p 333
[122] Nolan M. 'Anti-Americanism and Americanization in Germany' Politics and Society Vo. 33 No. 88 2005 p 92
[123] ibid

Republikaner and a fervent defender of economic and cultural protectionism for the sake of the 'small people,' argued against the American form of capitalism: "We want to say it the way it is: the golden years are over; we don't like big industry, and we don't want to be an American colony; our model is Bismarck."[124] Moreover, the process of standardization entailed in process of Americanisation is dangerous because "the one world of the economy would result in the one world of cultures, the leveling of differences and the *Gleichschaltung* of the people."[125] The process of Americanisation is corroding the traditional Western European model though the cuts in social provisions, the increased flexibility of the work force, and the alteration to wages due to a high level of competivity.

The New Right critique of both hypercapitalism and general standardisation attracts many sections of the population in Germany. The transformations within society brought about by economic globalisation has led to a rapid collapse of stability, to insecurity in performance at the workplace, to a sense of powerlessness in a era of fierce competition, and to feeling of isolation given by the break up of the family environment. A substantial part of the population finds it difficult to adapt to these radical transformations and seeks certainty, clarity and stability in order to overcome the state of insecurity. However, you also have those who take the opportunity to make use of the various advantages offered by globalisation. Dr. Barbara Wolf, former professor of special education in Dresden, has carried out several researches on the rise of far right extremisms. Wolf argues that, on the one hand, you find "well educated, possibly independent men and women, moving with self confidence between the various cultures, experience globalization as an opportunity and enlargement of their personal challenges."[126] Then, on the other hand, there are the 'losers of globalisation' with insufficient to no education, who lose their social remunerations and work prospective and are unable to live off their salary. Wolf mentions how in Saxony, one of major regions in Eastern Germany, there are areas with a high number of young, well-educated women who emigrated due to the lack of jobs, leaving behind poorly educated men and older people. For some of these people radical right wing parties start to become. Barbara Wolf's view is very similar to

---

[124] Schonhuber Franz in Betz Hans-Georg p 135
[125] Ibid
[126] Wolf B, former Professor of Special Education, 'Institut inform Dresden,' Phone Interview 2 May 2008

those of Mary Kaldor who affirmed that "typical recruits to these movements are the restless young men, often educated for roles that no longer exist because of the decline of the state or of the industrial sector, often unable to marry because they lack income….membership in nationalist groups offers meaning, a sense of historical relevance, and also adventure."[127] Moreover, the labour market requires mobility of the employee who should be willing to change their place of work, even abroad. This affects the family, which is seen as the nucleus of social life. Wolf also notes how if one looks at the development of income during the past years in Germany it becomes evident that the middle class income is under increasing burden and a large part of the middle class risks to significantly lose its status. She concludes by saying that although it is difficult to exactly determine the extent to which this condition influences an increase of radical right sentiments, it is obvious that it does.[128]

Many would argue against this perspective on the rise of the New Right by pointing to the last electoral results of the Republikaner. In the last years the German Republicans have been losing ground to neo-Nazi oriented parties such as the extreme right National Democratic Party (NPD) and the far-right German People's Union, both of which have repeatedly but in vainly attempted to convince the REP to join their electoral alliance. In the 2005 federal elections, the Republikaner obtained a mere 0.6 percent of the total national votes compared to the seven per cent received in the beginning of the 1990s.[129] However, if it is with no doubt evident that the main New Right party itself is not as successful as it has been in the past, the New Right discourse based on a nationalist ideology, which seeks a 'heterogeneous world of homogenous nations' in an era of increasing interconnectedness, has been adopted by many politicians of the Centre-Right CDU today in power. Previously it has been mentioned how many politicians of the mainstream CDU contribute to New Right publications. Moreover, Barbara Wolf points out how in the present CDU party there is a hidden radical right political orientation, which is not immediately evident and easy to determine, because those interrogated do not always openly admit to their opinion, as soon as they expect opposition: "the possibility of expressing personal attitudes openly can vary considerably as 'extremists' count on receiving approval by

---

[127] Kaldor M., 'Nationalism and Globalisation' p 169
[128] Wolf B interview
[129] 'Die Republikaner' www.rep.de Accessed on 10/04/08

the respective social environment or hesitate to express their personal opinion openly because they expect opposition."[130] Therefore, to answer the question if there has been a rise of New Right attitudes in Germany one must not only look at the electoral results because several factors have to be taken into account

---

[130] Barbara Wolf interview

Conclusion

The rise of New Right attitudes is not confined to the cases of Italy and Germany. In France, for example, Jean Marie Le Pen's Front National, a populist new right party which opposes neo-Gaullist ideals such as market liberalism and opposes multiculturalism on the notion that 'France is for the French', has been extremely successful in the past years due primarily to the fact that its political program has succeeded in bringing together different sections of the traditional, radical, extreme, and conservative Right. In the first round of the 2002 presidential election, the National Front shocked the whole country when it obtained a total of almost five million votes (16.86 per cent) which enabled Le Pen to beat the socialist candidate Lionel Jospin and advance to the second round, where he lost to Jacques Chirac by twenty million votes.[131] In the more recent national elections held last year, the *Front National* failed to repeat its previous success and did not manage to reach the second round, but still received around four million votes (10.44 per cent)[132], becoming the fourth most influential party out of twelve. Similarly to Bossi and Fini, one of Le Pen's primary concerns regards the consequences of economic and cultural globalisation. Indeed, Le Pen views market liberalism in a negative way because multinational companies and global financial enterprises were "only interested in getting maximum benefits at any price…including opening the doors to third-world immigrants in order to exploit their labour force, to the detriment of the latter, of European interests, and future European politics." [133] Multiculturalism and immigration in general are strongly opposed since they become "a major symptom of decadence, because it represents the acceptance of biological, ideological, and cultural mixing, the renunciation of traditions and the qualities which are particular to ethnic origins, and the abdication of the West."[134]

Jorg Haider in Austria, Pim Fortuyn in the Netherlands and many others across Europe have had similar if not more success in their respective countries. In the Austrian federal elections in 1999, Jorg Haider's Freedom Party gained twenty seven

---

[131] '2002 French Elections: Results at a Glance' BBC NEWS Online , Tuesday 23 April 2002 Accessed on 1/05/08 http://www.bbc.co.uk
[132] 'France opts for left-right battle' BBC NEWS Online, Monday 23 April 2007 Accessed on 1/05/08 http://www.bbc.co.uk
[133] Le Pen J.M. quoted in Betz H.G 'Radical Right Wing Populism in Western Europe' p 128
[134] Ibid p 130

per cent of the national vote! Indeed, it is safe to say that by the beginning of the twenty-first century it was possible to locate a radical right party in almost every Western European country and that in most of Western Europe, including Austria, Belgium, Denmark, France, Holland, Italy and Switzerland, a new right party has gained at least ten per cent of the vote.[135] The New Right ideology, therefore, is gaining increased support and its link with the concurrent strengthening of the processes of economic and cultural globalisation, the consequences of which are not being handled adequately enough by the mainstream governments, is not random. No doubt, the various processes entailed in globalisation are not the sole cause of financial instability, unemployment, fierce competition, immigration, the weakening of the nation state, the declining role of the family, the 'McDonaldization' of society, the hybridisation of cultures, the demise of traditional values, and a growing sense of uncertainty. Moreover, to assume that the only justifiable reason for the rise of New Right parties lies in the globalising of society would be simplistic and naïve. The 2008 Italian elections have shown how votes are frequently awarded to radical right parties as a protest against the current government, guilty of taking unpopular measures such as raising taxes. Le Pen's incredible success in the 2002 election was assisted by the extremely low turnout. A lot of the support for Pim Fortuyn came from 'Islamophobes' who felt insecure after the events of 9/11 and more importantly after the killing of the Dutch film maker Theo van Gogh, who was murdered by an Islamic fanatic after he had made a controversial film about Islam. Members of the Lega Nord and the Republikaner campaigned not only against economic and cultural globalisation but also in opposition to the European Union, arguing that too much sovereignty has been relocated to European Union institutions and that this has considerably undermined the role of the state: "too much daily life is controlled from Brussels and unelected bureaucrats determine policies."[136] The EU has been defined as 'Super Babylon' because it has compromised the sovereignty of its member states with the establishment of wide-ranging supranational decision-making institutions. Finally, the consolidation of radical right parties is also linked to a crisis of legitimacy and of confidence in the democratic system and the mainstream parties. In fact, Dalton shows how an "increasing public scepticism of political elites appears to be a

---

[135] Zaslove A. 'The Dark Side of European Politics: Unmasking the Radical Right' Journal of European Integration Vo. 26 No. 1 March 2004 p 62

[136] Sweeney S. 'Europe, the State and Globalisation' (2005, London: Pearson Education Limited) p 100

common development in many advanced industrial democracies" and how politicians and parties have often become the target of populist slogans of the radical right.[137] *Parteienverdrossenheit* (disaffection with party) has indeed become widespread in Germany and Italy.

The first reason for this disaffection is explained by the incapability of mainstream parties to fight the consequences of the socio-economic dynamics of globalisation. The New Right parties are thus the by-products of alienation at a deep level for government policies on the issues developed in a plural, multicultural, and globalising society. As Betz has pointed out, support for the populist right is "a reflection of the psychological strain produced by large-scale socio-economic and socio-structural change."[138] The success of the New Right is therefore fueled by the "failure of left and right wing governments successfully to address the problems of long term mass-unemployment, a crisis in the housing market arising from penury or deterioration of the existing a stock, and rising crime rates, have contributed to the revival of the radical right, which has tended to blame all three on immigration."[139]

The second reason for this growing disaffection with mainstream parties, and the consequent rise of the radical right, lies in the rise of party scandals involving corruption. In Italy the public's disbelief has reached unprecedented levels due to the continuous political scandals linked to corruption, which have affected the country over the past two decades. The most notorious and outrageous scandal involving key political figures occurred in the early 1990s when Mario Chiesa, a Socialist politician, was caught in Milan trying to get rid of thirty million lire (about ten thousand pounds) by flushing the money down the toilet. After his arrest, Chiesa admitted that he was only the tip of the iceberg by exposing the system of kickbacks, which caused top politicians such as Bettino Craxi and Giulio Andreotti to be put under investigation in what became known as 'Tangentopoli' ('bribeville').[140] The Mafia fought back against the maxi-trial by murdering both Giovanni Falcone and Paolo Borsellino, two key Italian magistrates who specialized in prosecuting members of the *Cosa Nostra*.

---

[137] Dalton R. 'Citizens Politics' (1996, Chatam:Chatam House) p 269
[138] Betz cited in Formisano R. 'Interpreting Right-Wing or Reactionary Neo-Populism: A Critique' Journal of Policy History Vo 17 No. 2 2005 p 244
[139] Meny Y. 'Government and Politics in Western Europe', revised by Knapp. A (1993, Oxford: Oxford University Press) p 63
[140] Ginsborg P., 'From Tangentopoli to Genoa', International Socialism Journal issue 95, 2002, p 1

The Observer published an article which perfectly described the state of Italy at that time: "Italy is in a state of war--it has the highest murder rate in the European Community, the most rampant and blatant corruption, an ailing economy, a floundering government, and an anguished and embarrassed population."[141] The population expressed its state of distrust by protesting in the streets, with fifty thousand people demonstrating in Milan and three hundred thousand rallying in Rome. Images of government leaders were burnt and slogans such as 'robbers' were shouted.[142]

Even Germany, often viewed as a model of honesty and incorruptibility, has not been exempt from political scandals. Indeed, at the beginning of the new century, Helmut Kohl, who had been German chancellor for over a decade, was the main protagonist of a financial scandal. Kohl, as chairman of the CDU, was forced to give his resignations when he admitted at a press conference, that he had "access to secret accounts from which he allotted large sums of money to individual representatives and party bodies, circumventing the responsible party structures and prevailing laws."[143] Later on, several revelations brought to light other suspicious financial dealings, such as the four hundred fifty million DM, which were partly used for commissions and bribes, which included almost everyone in the CDU leadership.[144] Certainly, corruption scandals like these contribute to the fact that more and more people feel abandoned, helpless and bewildered.

Yet, since the end of the Cold War the extraordinary acceleration of economic and cultural globalisation, eased by the international political context characterised by a unipolar world dominated by a hegemonic superpower, has introduced the most important and irreversible changes to which many Italians, Germans, and other Europeans have not managed to adapt quickly enough. Globalisation is a key post-industrial development, which has spread sentiments of uncertainty and displacement, creating as a consequence demands for identity and reassurance. Many people feel the need to be taken care of and want to be part of an aggregate, which can be provided

---

[141] The Observer quoted in Ginsborg p 2
[142] Ginsborg p 2
[143] Schwartz P. 'Financial Scandal envelops former German Chancellor Helmut Kohl' World Socialist Web Site, 4 December 1999, http://www.wsws.org Accessed on 10/04/08
[144] Ibid

by a common identity. As Paolo Ignazi pointed out, "only more radical parties can fully voice sentiments which reflect the demands for identity (hence nationalism), for homogeneity (hence xenophobia), and for order, hierarchy, and a strong leadership (hence authoritarianism)."[145] The New Right offers an alternative vision of the world based on the idea that we live in a world characterized by a plurality of unique nations, each with its own character and destiny, and therefore we should try to maintain and distinguish our identity because it gives the family extraordinary value and gives 'us' a sense of self-realisation through its promotion of unity, belonging, and self-sacrifice for the nation. Thus, the populist, charismatic, and original style of radical right leaders such as Umberto Bossi, who portray themselves as everyday, normal people by using a casual if not vulgar style of oration to oversimplify complex issues like immigration, has made it possible for New Right parties to substitute the traditional left-wing anti-globalisation movements by becoming electorally the most successful opponents of globalisation.

---

[145] Ignazi Piero 'Extreme Right Parties in Western Europe' (2003, Oxford: Oxford University Press) p 202

Bibliography

- Allesbacher Berichte, 'Multikulturelle Gesellschaft', No. 9 1992

- Antonucci Germano 'People of Freedoms triumphs-Northern League doubles vote' Corriere Della Sera 15 April 2008, http://www.corriere.it   Accessed on 15/04/08

- Assinder Nick 'Is Cameron the real power?' BBC News website 4 February 2008

- Baldini G. & Vignati R. 'Dal MSI ad AN: una nuova cultura politica?,'Polis, Vo.10 No.1 (1996)

- Baylis J. & Smith S. 'The Globalization of World Politics', (2005,Oxford: Oxford University Press)

- BBC NEWS Online, '2002 French Elections: Results at a Glance,' Tuesday 23 April 2002   Accessed on 1/05/08, http://www.bbc.co.uk

- BBC NEWS Online, 'France opts for left-right battle', Monday 23 April 2007 Accessed on 1/05/08 http://www.bbc.co.uk

- Beirich H. & Woods D. 'Globalisation, workers and the northern league' West European Politics Vo. 23 No. 1

- Betz Hans-Georg, 'Radical Right-Wing Populism in Western Europe' (London: The Macmillan Press, 1994)

- Brinks J.H, Rock S., Timms E., 'Nationalist Myths and Modern Media: Contested Identities in the Age of Identities' (2006, London:Tauris Academic Studies)

- Brubaker W.R. 'Citicenship and Nationhood in France and Germany' (1992, Cambridge, Mass: Harvard University Press)

- Business Week 'Germany: Is Reunification Failing?', November 15 1993

- Carnoy M., Castells M., Cohen S.S. and Cardoso F.H. 'The New Global Economy in the Information Age' (1993, University Park: The Pennsylvania State University Press)

- Cole J. 'The New Racism in Europe: A Sicilian ethnography' (1997, Cambridge: Cambridge University Press)

- CMtG, 'Nationalisten tegen Globalisering', available at: http://www.strijd.be/platform.htm Accessed on 10/01/08

- Dale H. C., 'Challenges Facing Europe in a World of Globalization', Heritage Lecture # 914,The Heritage Foundation, November 28, 2005

- Dalton R. 'Citizens Politics' (1996, Chatam:Chatam House)

- Danks Catherine J & Kennedy P.,'Globalization and National Identities: Crisis or Opportunity?' (2001, London: Palgrave)

- Diamanti Ilvo, 'Immigrazione e Cittadinanza in Europa'', Fondazione Nord Est, February 2001

- Die Republikaner, 'Die Republikaner' http://www.rep.de Accessed on 10/04/08

- EURISPES 1991 ,'Rapporto Italia 91' (Rome: Vallecchi Editore)

- European Parliament, 'Report of The Committe of Inquiry Into Racism and Xenophobia', European Parliament Session Documents 23 July 1990

- Evans Peter 'The Eclipse of the Sate? Reflections on Stateness in an Era of Globalization' World Politics Vol. 5.1 (1997)

- Fennema M., 'Some Theoretical Problems and Issues in Comparision of Anti-immigrant Parties in Western Europe', Working Paper no. 115 (Barcelona: Instituto de Ciencies Politiques I Socials 1996)

- GfK Press release, 'Anxiety about unemployment, concerns about inflation and fear of crime', Findings of the GfK survey, Challenges of Europe 2005

- Gingrich A. 'Neo-nationalism and the reconfiguration of Europe' Social Anthropology Vo. 14 No. 2 2006

- Ginsborg P., 'From Tangentopoli to Genoa', International Socialism Journal Issue 95, 2002

- Global Policy Forum 'US Market Share of Film Industry for Select Countries' http://www.globalpolicy.org Accessed on 17/03/08

- Graziano P., 'Europeanization or Globalization?', Global Social Policy, Vol 3 (2) Sage Pubblications

- Grund C. J. 'Euro-Gesellschaft statt Volk', Nation und Europa, Vo. 46 December 1996

- Hammar T. 'Comparing European and North American International Migration', International Migration Review Vo. 23 No. 3 1989

- Hebron L. & Stack J. F. 'TheGlobalization Process: Debunking the Myths.' Paper presented at the annual meeting of the International Studies Association, Chicago, 20-24 February 2001

- Held D. & McGrew A., 'Globalization/Anti-globalization' (2007, Cambridge: Polity Press)

- Held D., Mcgrew A., Goldblatt D., and Perraton J., 'Global Transformations' (1999, Cambridge: Polity Press)

- Hirst P. & Thompson G. 'Globalization in Question: The International Economy and the Possibilities of Governance' (1999, Cambridge: Polity Press)

- Hooper J. 'Italian right calls for repatriation of Roma', The Guardian Monday November 5 2007

- Huntington S., 'The Clash of Civilizations?' Foreign Affairs, Vol. 72, No 3 Summer 1973

- 'Globalization and Cultural Choice' Human Development Report 2004

- Ignazi Piero 'Extreme Right Parties in Western Europe' (2003, Oxford: Oxford University Press)

- Kaldor M., 'Nationalism and Globalisation', Nations and Nationalism Vol. 10 (1/2), 2004

- Kennedy P. & Danks C.J. 'Globalization and National Identities' (2001, London: Palgrave)

- Krauthammer C., 'Who Needs Gold Medals' Washington Post, February 20, 2002

- Krebs P. ,'Die europaische Wiedergeburt' (1982, Tubingen: Grabert)

- La Padania,'Un altro milione di immigrati? Saranno un'ottima forza-lavoro,' 21 June 2000

- La Republica, 'Martens: "Impossibile An in Ppe", Fini: "Solo opinioni personali"', 22 November 2006

- Lieber R. J. & Weisberg R. E., 'Globalization, Culture, and Identities in Crisis' , International Journal of Politics, Culture and Society, Vol. 16 No. 2, Winter 2002

- Melotti U 'L'immigrazione straniera in Italia;dati, cause, tipi'' Inchiesta 20 (October/December)

- Meny Y. 'Government and Politics in Western Europe', revised by Knapp. (1993,Oxford: Oxford University Press)

- Minkenberg M., 'German Unification and the Continuity of Discontinuities: Cultural Change and the Far Right in East and West', German Politics, Vol. 2 1994

- Mudde Cas 'Globalisation: The Multi-Faced Enemy?' CERC Working Papers Series No. 3/ 2004

- Nolan M. 'Anti-Americanism and Americanization in Germany' Politics and Society Vo. 33 No. 88 2005

- OECD, 'Trends in International Migration' (Geneva: OECD 2001)

- Pfahl-Traughber A., 'Rechtextremistische Intellektuelle gegen den demokratischen Verfassungsstaat' (1998, Opladen: Leske und Budrich)

- Pick D. 'The reflexive modernization of Australian Universities' Globalisation, Societies and Education, Vol. 2 , No 1, March 2004

- Rodman P., 'Uneasy Giant:The Challenges to American Predominance' (Washington DC, The Nixon Center, June 2002)

- Rothkop D. 'In praise of Cultural Imperialism? Effects of Globalization on Culture' Foreign Policy June 22, 1997

- Rosenberg, J. 'Globalization theory: a post-mortem', International Politics Vol. 42 (2), 2005

- Saul, J. R. 'The Collapse of Globalism', (2005, London: Atlantic Books)

- Schmitter H., 'A Comparative Perspective on the Underclass', Theory and Society Vo. 20 1991

- Scholte J. A. 'Globalization: a critical introduction' (2005, London: Palgrave Macmillan)

- Schroder R., 'Wie weit verbindet die Deutschen die gemeinsame Nation?', Wir Selbst, Vo. 3 No. 1999

- Schwartz P. 'Financial Scandal envelops former German Chancellor Helmut Kohl' World Socialist Web Site, 4 December 1999, http://www.wsws.org Accessed on 10/04/08

- Solomos J. & Wrench J. 'Race and Migration in Western Europe' (1993 Oxford: Berg Publishers Ltd)

- Spektorowski A., 'Ethnoregionalism: The Intellectual New Right and the Lega Nord,' <u>The Global Review of Ethnopolitics</u> Vo. 2 No.3 March 2003

- Stergios J. 'Language and Nationalism in Italy' <u>Nations and Nationalism</u> Vol 12 (1) 2006

- Strange S. 'The Defective State' <u>Daedalus</u> Vol.124 (Spring 1995)

- Sweeney S. 'Europe, the State and Globalisation' (2005, London: Pearson Education Limited)

- Ter Wal J. 'The Discourse of the Extreme Right and its Ideological Implications: The Case of the Alleanza Nazionale on Immigration' <u>Patterns of Prejudice</u> Vo. 34 No. 4, 1 October 2000

- The Committee on Intellectual Correspondance, 'Globalization and Cinema : An International Review of Culture and Society', <u>Council on Foreign Relations</u>, No. 8 Summer/Fall 2001

- <u>The Economist,</u> 'Alitalia: Rapid Descent,' March 22nd 2008

- <u>The Economist,</u> 'A World Empire By Other Means,'(London), December 22 2001

- <u>The Economist,</u> 'Italy's election: Promises, but no delivery,' March 29th 2008

- <u>The Economist,</u> 'Two unamalgamated worlds', April 5th 2008

- The Pew Research Center, 'What the World thinks in 2002,' <u>Pew Global Attitudes Project</u>, December 4 2002

- UN Chronicle, '"Diplomacy can be effective', says Secretary-General Interview,", Spring, 1998

- Warnier J. P. 'La mondialisation de la culture'(2003 Paris : Edition la Decouverte')

- Wiesberg M. 'Der Westen muss sich wehren', <u>Junge Freiheit</u>, 6 September 2002

- Wolf B, former Professor of Special Education, 'Institut inform Dresden,' Phone Interview 2 May 2008

- WTO-2 (1996b) 'Ruggiero Calls for Trading System to be Kept in Line with Globalization Process'. WTO press release, 22 February

- Zaslove A. 'The Dark Side of European Politics: Unmasking the Radical Right' <u>Journal of European Integration</u> Vo. 26 No. 1 March 2004